Titles in the series:

The Duck 0-241-11466-7
The Fox 0-241-11215-X
The Hedgehog 0-241-11467-5
The Mouse 0-241-11213-3
The Owl 0-241-11468-3
The Pigeon 0-241-11214-1
The Squirrel 0-241-11216-8
The Starling 0-241-11469-1

Design by Linda Rogers Associates

First Published in Great Britain 1985 by
Hamish Hamilton Children's Books
Garden house, 57 – 59 Long Acre, London WC2E 9JZ
Copyright © 1985 by Joyce Pope
Copyright © Illustrations 1985 by Elizabeth Goss

British Library Cataloguing in Publication Data
Pope, Joyce
The hedgehog.—(Animals in towns)
1. Hedgehogs—Juvenile literature
2. Urban fauna—Juvenile literature
I. Title   II. Goss, Elizabeth   III. Series
599.3′3   QL737.I53
ISBN 0-241-11467-5

Printed in Great Britain by
Blantyre Printing and Binding Ltd
London and Glasgow

Animals in Towns

The Hedgehog

Joyce Pope

Illustrated by Elizabeth Goss

Hamish Hamilton · London

The big berberis bush near the gates of the town park looked beautiful when it was in flower. Everybody said so – which is perhaps why it was never cut back. People often stopped to watch the bees feeding on the golden, nectar-full flowers. But nobody noticed the big pile of dead leaves that seemed to be caught below the drooping spiny branches. Nor did they see the little creature which had slept through the winter in this dry, sheltered spot.

One warm afternoon in early April, anyone who had been watching would have seen the leaves begin to stir, almost as if they were breathing. By tea-time a sharp little black nose had appeared, followed by a grey furry face with two bright black eyes, looking out on a world they had not seen since last autumn. By the time most people were eating supper,

the spiny-backed hedgehog had emerged completely from her winter nest and was out hunting for her first meal of the year.

It was quite dark in the park, but this didn't bother the hedgehog. She relied mainly on her sense of smell to tell her about her surroundings. She walked quite slowly across the flower-bed and path, and on to the football pitch where the scent of trampled grass filled her nostrils.

Suddenly a new smell caught her attention and she changed course to follow the track of a beetle. Many animals would have left it alone for it had a very strong and unpleasant odour, but the hedgehog didn't mind and soon scrunched it up. Yet one beetle is not very much for a hungry hedgehog , and the first was soon followed by a second and a third and some millipedes.

The hedgehog zigzagged her way across the field in search of food. But although her path looked aimless, she was in fact heading for the wire fence which surrounded the field. She had remembered that part of it was loose enough for her to squeeze underneath. On the other side was the large overgrown garden of one of the old houses bordering the park. Here, in a vegetable plot, she feasted on little black slugs until she could eat no more.

In her night's hunting she had travelled nearly two kilometres and she was tired. So she burrowed into an untidy pile of dead vegetation near the bottom of the garden, and slept through the day.

Throughout the next month the hedgehog looked for food at night and slept during the day. She was not the only animal to be out hunting. She shared the park and the gardens with scavenging cats and a pair of town foxes. But although she was much smaller than these animals, she was quite unafraid.

One night, a fox, searching for food for his mate and their new cubs, sniffed at her. He was far too cautious to attack her directly. As he approached, the hedgehog rolled herself up into a tight ball so that her spines, which normally lay flat like thick hairs over her back, stood out sharply in all directions. The fox didn't know what to do. He stood for a moment, his nose tingling where the spines had pricked it, then ran off to look for easier food in the town.

When he had gone, the hedgehog slowly uncurled. She took no chances, in case there was still an enemy about. But in town a hedgehog is safe from most other animals, and the fox never bothered her again.

Sometimes the hedgehog hunted for food in the churchyard. To get there, she had to leave the park and cross the road. Normally, there was very little traffic, but if she did hear a car or a lorry she would curl up into a spiny ball. She did not understand that motors are not afraid of sharp spines. Once she had a narrow escape when the wheels of a car passed on either side of her, but luckily she survived.

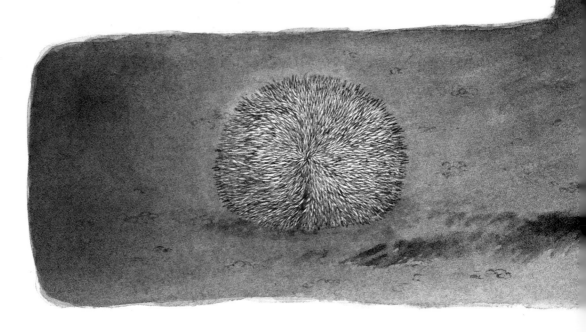

As the weather began to get warmer, the hedgehog found enough food close by. There were plenty of caterpillars and other insect grubs, and several families put out saucers of bread and milk and sometimes a few bacon rinds for her in their gardens. The hedgehog liked milk and would lick the dishes quite clean. Each family called her "our hedgehog" as none of them realised how far she travelled to get her food.

Although the families watched her feeding, they were careful not to touch her in case they frightened her. Also, they knew that all hedgehogs have fleas and other parasites. Their spines make it difficult for them to groom themselves and get rid of such pests. And though the fleas can only survive on hedgehogs, nobody wants such a guest, for even a short visit!

Each night the hedgehog wandered several kilometres in search for food, snuffling among leaves and round the base of plants for any small creature she could find. Slugs and grubs and insects – she ate them all. One night, in the long grass in the churchyard, she found a nest of very young voles, which she quickly dug out and ate. She didn't often get the chance of such a feast, for though she often came across the tracks of mice and shrews, they were generally quick enough to get out of her way.

10

Another night in the park, she discovered an ice-cream tub which a boy had dropped. She had never met such a thing before, but the smell was quite delicious. She stuck her head into the pot to lick the smears left at the bottom. When she had cleaned every bit, she tried to pull her head out of the carton. But what a dreadful shock she had! The spines at the back of her head caught on the rim and she was trapped, unable to see or smell where she was going. Wildly she scraped at the awful thing with her long claws, and finally tore it so that she was able to free herself. But she had had a narrow escape, and it was lucky for her that she found no more tubs or tins.

During the day, the hedgehog slept in one of several nests she had made of dead grass and leaves. Which one she chose mainly depended on how far she had gone in her night's hunting. At night the paths she took often criss-crossed those used by other hedgehogs. She recognised their scent, but ignored them; she was not a sociable animal and had no need of other hedgehogs' company.

One night in mid May, as she was searching near the compost heap in one of her gardens, she met a male hedgehog whose living space overlapped with hers. Her

sense of smell told her that he too was one of the inhabitants of the park and gardens. But instead of ignoring her, he walked towards her, almost as if he were going to bump into her. She turned away, but he changed course, so that again he was walking towards her. She grunted as she turned away once more, but it was no good. The male continued to circle her, puffing and snorting to match the noise that she was making. Each time she tried to avoid him he simply circled closer, so that soon they were going round in tighter and tighter circles.

14

All this snorting and grunting soon attracted another hedgehog. The newcomer approached very close as though he wanted to join in. But as soon as the first male spotted the intruder he stopped hustling the female and turned to face the stranger. He then butted the second hedgehog on the head.

It was not a very fierce or long battle for as soon as her suitor turned away, the female hurried across the flower-beds and grass and under the fence into another garden. She was not yet ready to mate. The two rivals continued to push at each other until they realised that they had nothing to fight over, then they too went their separate ways.

Several nights later the hedgehog met the same male and again they circled round and round in a small ring. This time, though, they were on a lawn close to a house. The people who lived there wondered what the strange noise could be, and went outside with a torch to see what was making such a disturbance. The hedgehogs were upset by the light suddenly shining on them, and rolled up into tight prickly balls. Then when everybody had gone back inside, they went off in opposite directions.

Two nights later they met again, this time in the park. Now there was nobody to hear the noise they made as they shuffled round in their slow-motion dance. Eventually the female stood quite still, her spines completely flattened so that the male could mate with her.

Very soon afterwards, the male went on his way and she continued with her normal night's hunting. Hedgehogs do not have a settled family life like that of many other animals. During the next week the hedgehog met and mated with several other males, but none of them remained with her for more than a few hours.

Towards the middle of June the hedgehog began to collect pieces of dry grass and dead leaves. She carried them to a snug, dry spot well protected by a thick hedge in one of the overgrown gardens.

It isn't always easy to find dry vegetation in the middle of the summer, but the town hedgehog had other things in use. Near to the litter bins in the park, she found some paper tissues and old toffee papers that people had dropped. She carried them carefully back to the hedge and pushed them into the pile of dead leaves. Eventually, she made a large, warm nest which was to be her nursery.

There, one morning in late June, her five babies were born. The baby hedgehogs did not look a bit like their mother. Their faces were short, their eyes tightly shut, and they had no spines – only tiny bumps on the greyish skin of their backs. The rest of their bodies were bright pink. Their mother gave them milk and the babies grew fast. Soon the bumps grew into softish, white spines.

19

When the babies were about a week old, sharp brown spines began to appear through their skin. These got bigger and bigger until they quite hid the little white prickles underneath. Their skin began to darken, and by the time they were two weeks old, their eyes had opened and they could see. Their mother went out each night to hunt for food, but the babies had to stay quietly in the nest, for they were still too small to feed on anything but milk.

One warm night, when they were nearly four weeks old, the hedgehog took them out of their snug nursery for the first

time. She led them across the garden to where a bowl of milk was waiting. The babies snuffled and snorted and got the milk up their noses but still managed to drink quite a lot. Then she led them to the flower-bed where they found beetles and slugs. On that first night they were very clumsy at catching anything, but they got better and were soon able to do without their mother's milk.

After another ten nights or so they left the nest and went their own ways. It was mid summer and there was plenty of food so even not very good hunters could survive.

Without her family, the hedgehog could concentrate on finding food for herself. The days were already becoming shorter, but it was still warm and there was plenty to eat. She gorged herself on worms and grubs until she became very fat.

When the first leaves turned brown and fell from the trees, the hedgehog started to collect mouthfuls of the dry vegetation. She chose several places to make warm, secure shelters. A protected spot by a sagging fence was one; another was beneath the thorny branches of an old rose bush.

When the first really cold nights came in late October and there was hardly any food, she remained curled up in her bed, secure in the deep sleep of hibernation. Anyone who had seen her, would have thought she was dead. She was hardly breathing, her body was cold, and her heart was beating very, very slowly.

Yet she was in fact alive, living on the fat beneath her skin. And the nest would keep her from freezing, even when there was thick frost and snow outside. One day , next April, the leaves would stir again and the hedgehog would come back out into the park and gardens of the town.

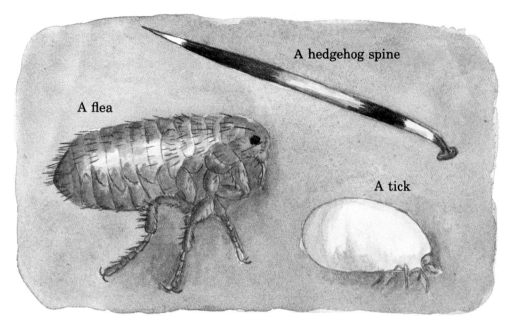

A hedgehog spine

A flea

A tick

Everthing in this book is true. Hedgehogs live in lots of
towns, feeding on the insects, worms and other small
creatures they can find in parks and gardens and on waste
ground, even in the middle of big cities. One way you might
find out they are there is by seeing the remains of
hedgehogs killed on the road. Many hedgehogs die this way.

If you think there are live hedgehogs about, listen for them
at night. They are not afraid of anything and so they are
often noisy. If you put out a saucer of milk, you may find
that the hedgehog has adopted you. Then you can have a
real wild friend. It won't be one you can touch or stroke, but
you can still find out a lot about it. See what sorts of food it
likes. Try to discover where its nest is and if you have a
garden, leave a bit of it wild so that the hedgehog may be
sure of safe place to hunt and to hibernate.

◀ Be careful that hedgehogs do not hibernate in your bonfire